THE DARK HISTORY OF MOTHER'S DAY

The Shocking Tragic Facts About Mother's Day That You Should Know

Anna Sleek

INTRODUCTION

Why Make Handmade Mom Gifts?

Individualized pillow

Make a Silhouette Brooch Create personalized brooches.

Ceramic Mugs Make Great Mother's Day Gifts

Customized Notepads

Stamps and cards made by hand

Write Mom Heartfelt Letters

Personalized monogram

Soaps with scents to help Mom unwind

Scarf with Style

INTRODUCTION

Have you ever wondered why we celebrate Mother's Day and where it began? We go into the history of the tradition as well as some interesting facts. The best friend and supporter anyone can have is one's mother. They've always had our backs, from nurturing us as children to staying with us as cranky teenagers and providing the occasional shoulder to cry on. This is why we celebrate Mother's Day every year all throughout the world.

Though the practice dates back several centuries, it has remained a significant occasion on the calendar, with unique store-bought or homemade Mother's Day cards, flowers, and large Mothering Sunday presents. We provide some fascinating facts about how the festival developed to help you prepare for Mother's Day and perhaps inspire some Mother's Day activities.

Because Mother's Day has a variety of roots, different countries celebrate it on different days of the year. Maternal and motherhood celebrations date back to the ancient Greeks and Romans. Mother worship was practiced in ancient Greece, including a festival dedicated to Cybele, the great mother of Greek gods. Cybele was a Phrygian goddess who originated in Anatolian mythology and whose worship expanded throughout ancient Greece and the Roman Empire. She was a goddess of fertility, nature, caverns and mountains, as well as walls and strongholds, and she represented Mother Earth.

From the Ides of March (March 15) to March 18, this festival was observed around the Vernal Equinox in Asia Minor and eventually in Rome. Matronalia, another ancient Roman feast dedicated to Juno, was observed on this day, albeit mothers were generally given gifts.

The clearest modern precedent for Mother's Day is the early Christian feast known as "Mothering Sunday." This feast, which came on the fourth Sunday in Lent and was originally considered a time when the faithful would return to their "mother church"—the principal church in their home region—for a particular service, was formerly a common practice in the United Kingdom and parts of

Europe. Over time, Mothering Sunday evolved into a more secular festival, with children presenting flowers and other tokens of gratitude to their mothers. In the 1930s and 1940s, this ritual declined in prominence before combining into American Mother's Day.

The modern-day Mother's Day celebration began in 1908 when Anna Jarvis created a memorial for her mother, Ann Jarvis, a peace campaigner who used to care for wounded Civil War troops. The ceremony was hosted at the International Mother's Day Shrine, which is currently housed in St Andrew's Methodist Church in Grafton, West Virginia. Anna Jarvis set out to garner support for the commemoration of Mother's Day in the United States after her mother died the same year. She wanted to pay tribute to all the mothers around the world who have made significant contributions to their families and society.

Because of her tireless efforts, most US states began commemorating Mother's Day as a municipal holiday in 1911, and West Virginia, Jarvis' home state, was the first to do so in 1910. The second Sunday in May was officially established as Mother's Day in the United States after Woodrow Wilson, the 28th President of the United States of America, signed the proclamation in 1914.. As a result, the current Mother's Day was born in the United States, and countries including India, Bangladesh, Pakistan, Italy, Singapore, Belgium, and many others have chosen the same date.

CHAPTER ONE

MOTHER'S DAY IN THE MODERN ERA

The origins of Mother's Day and the commemoration of motherhood trace back to the Ancient Greeks. At their spring celebration, they celebrated the goddess Rhea, also known as the Mother of the Gods. Rhea was related to Cybele, another mother goddess revered by the Romans.

It wasn't always Mother's Day, but rather a time during Lent when people returned to their mother church, the main church, for a special ceremony.

This is why every year on the fourth Sunday of Lent, Mother's Day is honored every year on the second Sunday of May. Families reuniting at this Mothering Sunday service also inspired the gift-giving practice. The kids would collect flowers and offer bouquets to their mothers on their way to church. As a result, online flower delivery is still the preferred Mother's Day gift today.

In the middle ages, apprentices and servants were given Mothering Sunday off to spend with their mothers. They'd bring a Simmer cake, a special Mother's Day dessert. There were almond paste layers in the center and on top, along with 11 marzipan balls to represent Jesus' apostles (excluding Judas Iscariot).

Mother's Day celebrations dropped in popularity in the 1900s, but were revived in the twentieth century because to the efforts of an American woman named Anna Jarvis.

Mother's Day became an official American holiday in 1914 as a result of Jarvis' lobbying of President Woodrow Wilson.

THE FAMOUS FOUNDER OF MOTHERS DAY, ANNA JARVIS

The story of Mother's Day is about a daughter, Anna Jarvis, who was determined to honor her mother, Mrs. Anna M Jarvis, and all other mothers around the world. Anna Jarvis dedicated her life to realizing her mother's ambition of having a day set aside to honor mothers. Despite never having been a mother, Anna Jarvis, the founder of Mother's Day, is now known as the "Mother of Mother's Day." A fitting phrase for the extraordinary woman's unwavering loyalty to her mother and parenthood in general.

Childhood

Anna Jarvis was born on May 1, 1864, in Webster, Taylor County, West Virginia. Ann Marie and Granville Jarvis had eleven children, and she was the eighth. When Anna was a year old, her family relocated to Grafton. Anna received her education in this location. She enrolled at the Augusta Female Academy, now Mary Baldwin College, in Staunton, Virginia, in 1881. Anna returned to Grafton after finishing her studies and taught in a school for seven years.

Inspiration for Mother's Day

Anna Jarvis was inspired to celebrate Mother's Day early in her life. Mrs. Jarvis, Anna's mother, said a class prayer in the presence of her daughter one day when Anna was 12 years old. Mrs. Jarvis made a little prayer at the end of the 'Mothers of the Bible' lesson, "I hope that someday someone can develop a memorial mother's day to honor her for her unmatched contribution to humanity in all areas of life. She has a right to it."

This was a prayer Anna never forgot. "...by the grace of God, you shall have that Mother's Day," she stated at her Mother's funeral service, recalling the prayer. Her brother, Claude, overheard the words.

Mother's Day: The Battle

Anna Jarvis determined to commemorate her mother after her mother died in 1905. When she discovered that adult children in the United States were neglectful of their parents, she became even more committed to her goal. Anna's judgments were strengthened by her mother's wish that someone would one day pay honor to all moms, living and deceased, and appreciate their efforts.

Miss Anna initiated an intensive push to establish a National Mother's Day in the United States in 1907. She led a brief homage to her mother at Andrews Methodist Church on the second anniversary of her mother's passing. Mother's Day was honored in her hometown of Philadelphia the following year.

Miss Anna Jarvis and her friends began writing hundreds of letters to persons in positions of authority advocating for a national Mother's Day to give shape to her goal. Anna, a native speaker, took advantage of every opportunity to promote her cause. Though the reception was initially lukewarm, she was able to break through by enlisting the help of Philadelphia merchant and philanthropist John Wanamaker. With his help, the movement received new momentum.

In 1909, forty-five states honored the day with appropriate services, including Puerto Rico, Hawaii, Canada, and Mexico. People also wore white and red Carnations to honor their mothers, as Anna Jarvis had initiated the practice. Carnations were Anna's first choice because they were her mother's favorite flower. Her favorite flower was the white carnation, which symbolized the purity of a mother's heart. A red carnation was to be worn to honor a living mother and a white carnation to honor a deceased mother.

Mother's Day was observed in practically every state of the Union by 1911. In 1914, President Woodrow Wilson issued an official proclamation designating Mother's Day as a national holiday to be observed annually on the second Sunday in May.

Why Do We Celebrate Mother's Day?

Anna Jarvis, an outspoken campaigner, walked outside the house's four walls. Her demeanor is notable in that she does not look down on traditional ladies who are content to stay at home. Instead, she worked to give honor and dignity to women who worked at home. One of her key goals in commemorating Mother's Day was to do this. Mother's Day is designed to honor the woman who gave us life and gave us birth. Though we frequently express gratitude to our mothers, we do not always express it. Mother's Day is observed to express our feelings toward our mothers. Spending quality time with her and making her feel special. Those who are separated from their mothers must write or call them to express their thoughts of love and thanks.

Her Dissatisfaction with the Commercialization of Mother's Day

It's worth noting that, after dedicating her life to the development of national Mother's Day, Miss Anna Jarvis was ultimately unsatisfied with the outcome. She was more concerned with reform than with money. She despised the commercialization of the day, to the point where she regretted even creating the Mother's Day tradition.

Anna died on November 24, 1948, at the age of 84. She is buried with her mother in Philadelphia's West Laurel Hill Cemetery. The bell on the Andrews Church in Grafton was tolled eighty-four times in her honor on the day of her interment. Four miles south of Grafton is the Anna Jarvis Birthplace Museum.

Mrs. Ann Marie Reeves Jarvis, her mother

Anna Jarvis' story Mrs. Anna M. Jarvis had 11 children, but only four of them survived to adulthood. Mrs. Jarvis maintained an active life despite her huge family. She was active in church and civic activities on a regular basis. The establishment of Mother's Day Work Clubs in local churches was a significant contribution to the society in which she lived. Mrs. Anna Jarvis urged the women of Webster, Philippi, Pruntytown, Fetterman, and Grafton to join the club in order to address the poor health and sanitation conditions that plagued their community at the time, contributing to the high child death rate. The clubs were a huge success, and everyone recognized their contribution to solving a local community problem.

Mrs Anna Jarvis asked members of Mother's Day Work Clubs to take a neutral stance during the Civil War and nurse both Union and Confederate soldiers. The Jarvis family eventually relocated to Grafton, West Virginia, near the end of the war.

Anna Jarvis hosted a Mothers' Friendship Day at Pruntytown Courthouse in 1865, following the Civil War. This was done to bring soldiers and neighbors from various political backgrounds together. The event was a huge success, and it has since been held annually to promote peace and friendship for numerous years.

Mrs. Anna Jarvis was an active churchgoer as well. When the Andrews Methodist Episcopal Church school was finished in 1873, she took leadership of the primary department. She taught the school's kids for more than two decades. Mrs. Jarvis was also a well-known public speaker in her day. Her sermons were well-received in the church.

Ann Marie Reeves Jarvis relocated to Philadelphia with her daughters, Anna and Lillie, following the loss of her husband, Granville E. Jarvis, in 1902. Mrs. Jarvis died on May 9, 1905, at the age of 72. She was laid to rest in Philadelphia's West Laurel Hill Cemetery. Andrews Methodist Episcopal Church in Grafton tolled the bell seventy-two times in her honor on the day she was laid to rest.

CHAPTER TWO

JULIA WARD HOWE

Mothering Sunday, an already-existing Christian ecclesiastical holiday in which the faithful visit the church where they received the sacrament of baptism, was proposed as an alternative by Constance Adelaide Smith.

She mentioned medieval celebrations of Mother Church, "mothers of earthly households," Mary, Jesus' mother, and Mother Nature. Her efforts in the British Isles and other English-speaking countries were effective.

From her Mother's Day Peace Proclamation. Few people realize that the first proponents of Mother's Day in the United States envisioned it as a day of peace to recognize and support mothers who had lost sons and husbands in the Civil War's carnage.

Julia Ward Howe, a social justice advocate, issued her inspired Mother's Day Proclamation in 1870, nearly 40 years before it became an official US holiday in 1914, calling on women of all nations to unite to support "amicable settlement of international questions, the broad and general interests of peace." She envisioned a solemn council day where women from all around the world might gather to debate how to achieve world peace.

Julia Ward Howe was an abolitionist, feminist, poet, and the author of "The Battle Hymn of the Republic," among other works.

During the civil war, she cared for the wounded and worked with the widows and orphans of troops on both sides, aware that the war's consequences extend well beyond the slaughter of men in battle. She used the damage she saw during the civil war to urge for women to "stand up through the ashes and devastation," advocating for a Mother's Day dedicated to peace. Her campaigning continued when the Franco-Prussian War resurfaced in the world.

With the help of Anna Jarvis, who was inspired by her mother, also named Anna Jarvis, who had worked with Julia Ward Howe in earlier efforts for a Mother's Day, the call for a Mother's Day acquired new momentum and eventually became a national holiday in the early 1900s.

While Mother's Day has lost much of its early edge for justice, we should remember some of the underlying ideals and recommit ourselves to its prophetic mission. It's time for Mother's Day to return to its roots at a time when our country is once again embroiled in costly and destructive wars abroad, and many of our own neighborhoods are torn apart by violence.

In the spirit of Ward Howe's original plea, we can use this occasion to commit ourselves, on behalf of all mothers, fathers, sisters, and brothers, to stand up and protect our most vulnerable by calling on our leaders to change the trajectory of our country. There is no greater need than to combat the damage caused by violence in all of its forms, which affects the lives of millions of people in our country and around the world.

Then, perhaps, the carnage and devastation of violence and war will finally vanish into history.

Of course, there is no better way to thank our mothers than this.

Social Activism by Julia Ward Howe

Julia Ward Howe's Biography Julia was influenced by William Lloyd's anti-slavery group during the 1850s. When the war broke out, she and her husband worked for the Sanitary Commission.

Julia Ward Howe and Caroline Severance created the New England Woman's Club in 1868. She also began attending meetings of the New England Woman Suffrage Association, which she led from 1868 to 1877 and 1893 to 1910. She and Lucy Stone co-founded the American Woman Suffrage Association in 1869. She also served as president of the Massachusetts Suffrage Association from 1870 to 1878 and 1891 to 1893, and contributed significantly to Lucy Stone's Woman's Journal. Julia's perspective was altered as a result of these actions. She began to view womanhood in a more favorable light.

Julia launched a one-woman peace crusade during the Franco-Prussian war in the 1870s, making an emotional "appeal to ladies" to rise up against war. She had her powerful Mother's Day Proclamation (written in Boston in 1870) translated into various languages and extensively published. In 1872, Julia Ward Howe traveled to London to promote an international Woman's Peace Congress. She started a Mothers' Peace Day event on the second Sunday in June in Boston and held it for several years. She fought hard for the official recognition of Mother's Day and the proclamation of the day as a national holiday.

Her suggestion was well received, but the Mother's Day celebration, which is now celebrated in May, eventually took its place.

Julia traveled the country giving lectures and forming women's clubs. In 1893, he delivered a speech titled "What Is Religion?" at the World Parliament of Religions in Chicago. Julia Ward Howe was elected to the American Academy of Arts and Letters for the first time in 1908.

On October 17, 1910, Julia Ward Howe died. At ceremonies held at the Church of the Disciples and Symphony Hall, a big crowd gathered to pay their respects to the pioneering woman in writing.

Julia Ward Howe is the subject of several biographies, and her name also appears in the 'Notable American Women' and 'American National Biography' collections.

CHAPTER THREE

INTERNATIONAL TRADITION, HISTORY AND CELEBRATION

Mother's Day is still commemorated in the United States by giving gifts and flowers to moms and other women, and it has become one of the most expensive holidays for consumers. Families frequently honor moms by giving them a day off from household responsibilities such as cooking.

Mother's Day has occasionally been used to promote political or feminist concerns. In 1968, Coretta Scott King, Martin Luther King Jr.'s wife, held a march in support of disadvantaged mothers and children on Mother's Day. In the 1970s, women's organizations utilized the occasion to emphasize the importance of equal rights and access to childcare.

While Mother's Day is celebrated in various ways around the world, customs differ by country. Mother's Day is always observed in August in Thailand, on the birthday of the current queen, Sirikit. Antrosht, a multi-day celebration honoring mothers, brings Ethiopian families together each fall to sing songs and enjoy a big feast.

On February 2, Afghanistan celebrates Mother's Day, Armenia on March 8, Armenia on April 7, Spain on the first Sunday in May, Mongolia (Mother's and Children's Day) on June 1, Costa Rica on August 15 (Assumption Day), Malawai on the second Monday in October, Russia on the last Sunday in November, and Panama on December 8.

The scale of the festivities varies tremendously. In certain nations, failing to commemorate Mother's Day may be considered insulting to one's mother. In some places, it's a little-known event attended primarily by immigrants, or it's covered by the media as a sample of foreign culture.

Mother's Day is a relatively new commemoration in most nations, deriving from the holiday's evolution in North America and Europe. Many African countries embraced the British practice of a single Mother's Day, despite the fact that there are other festivals and celebrations honoring mothers across the African continent that predate colonization. Other countries have created their own Mother's Day traditions based on their own cultures.

Japan

In Japan, Mother's Day was first observed as Empress Kjun's birthday during the Shwa period (1926–1989). (mother of Emperor Akihito). The festival is now widely commercialized, much like in the United States, and individuals commonly send flowers such as carnations and roses as gifts.

China

In recent years, some in China have advocated for the official recognition of Mother's Day in honor of Meng Mu, Mèng Z's mother (371–289 B.C.E.). Except in a few cities, it is still an unofficial festival.

Greece

In Greece, Mother's Day coincides with the Eastern Orthodox feast of the Presentation of Jesus at the Temple. This feast is associated with women since the Theotokos (Mother of God) featured prominently in it as the one who carried Christ to the Temple in Jerusalem.

CHAPTER FOUR

THE MOTHERS DAY FOUNDER HATE THE HOLIDAY SHE CREATED

Anna Jarvis, the woman who started Mother's Day in 1908, was a vocal opponent of the holiday's rising commercialization who eventually fought against it.

Mother's Day was created by Anna Jarvis, who had no children of her own, to recognize the sacrifices made by individual mothers for their children. She planned the first formal Mother's Day activities in Grafton, West Virginia, and at a Wanamaker's department store in Philadelphia, where she lived at the time.

Jarvis then began writing letters to newspapers and lawmakers, requesting that Mother's Day be become a national holiday. By 1912, Mother's Day had spread to many more churches, municipalities, and states, and Jarvis had founded the Mother's Day International Association. In 1914, President Woodrow Wilson signed a measure designating the second Sunday in May as Mother's Day, putting an end to her long battle.

Jarvis saw Mother's Day as a personal celebration—a son or daughter celebrating the mother they knew and loved—rather than a national holiday. As a result, she constantly emphasized the singular "Mother's" above the plural. Mother's Day quickly became oriented on the purchase and gifting of printed cards, flowers, candies, and other presents, and she became disillusioned.

Jarvis began openly fighting against those who benefitted from Mother's Day, including confectioners, florists, and other shopkeepers, in order to reclaim control of the holiday she invented. She filed multiple lawsuits against organizations that used the phrase Mother's Day, and she finally spent a large portion of her inheritance on legal bills.

Jarvis was jailed for breaking the peace in Philadelphia in 1925, when an organization called the American War Mothers exploited Mother's Day as a fundraising and carnation-selling opportunity.

She went on to criticize First Lady Eleanor Roosevelt for using Mother's Day to generate money for charity. By the 1940s, Jarvis had completely abandoned the holiday, even lobbying the government to have it deleted from the calendar. Mother's Day had taken on a life of its own as a commercial goldmine, so her efforts were futile. Jarvis died at Philadelphia's Marshall Square Sanitarium in 1948, largely destitute and unable to profit from the immensely profitable holiday she founded.

The tragic past of Mother's Day creator Anna Jarvis has had no effect on the holiday's popularity—or commercialism. According to the National Retail Federation's annual shopping study, Americans spent an average of $168.94 on Mother's Day in 2013, an increase of 11% over 2012.

According to the National Retail Foundation, annual Mother's Day spending tops $20 billion. In addition to more traditional gifts (such as cards, flowers, and chocolates, as well as clothing and jewelry), one survey found that 14.1 percent of gift-givers plan to buy their mothers high-tech gadgets such as smartphones and tablets.

CHAPTER FIVE

WHY IS MOTHER'S DAY CELEBRATED MORE THAN FATHER'S DAY?

Have you forgotten about Father's Day yet? You're not by yourself. Take a look at the figures. To be clear, this is not an argument that Mother's Day should be prioritized for everyone. It's a reflection on my own personal experience as well as an investigation into the cultural significance of Mother's Day. Dad, I apologize.

Here are a few reasons why I believe Mother's Day is more widely observed than Father's Day.

Have you ever celebrated Mother's Day by dining out? You very certainly have, and you almost certainly waited an inordinate amount of time for a table. I've worked at a restaurant on Mother's Day for my whole working life, and let me tell you, it's an awful disaster.

Why is Mother's Day so much more significant than Father's Day?

While this may not be true for everyone, it is certainly true for me. I wanted to spend some time thinking about why Mother's Day is so important to me, and why it appears to be increasingly culturally significant as well.

To be clear, this is not an argument that Mother's Day should be prioritized for everyone. It's a reflection on my own personal experience as well as an investigation into the cultural significance of Mother's Day. Dad, I apologize.

Have you ever celebrated Mother's Day by dining out? You very certainly have, and you almost certainly waited an inordinate amount of time for a table. I've worked at a restaurant on Mother's Day for my whole working life, and let me tell you, it's an awful disaster.

Where I worked, Mother's Day was clearly the busiest day of the year, with Thanksgiving quickly gaining a place. Every employee looks forward to this day of the year. There isn't a single moment of respite throughout the day. It's basically crazy from start to finish. Father's Day, on the other hand, occurs on a Sunday in June.

Why is Mother's Day so much more popular than Father's Day for eating out?

The traditional role of the woman and mother, which is to cook for the family, is a potential cause. As a result, families are more inclined to eat out to give her a break from the kitchen. However, there are many families for whom this is not the case, so why do individuals continue to eat out in spite of the horrendous crowds? I think what I'm trying to say is that people ought to stop going out on Mother's Day every single year. It isn't worthwhile. Instead, prepare a meal for her.

Money speaks, and money still says Mother's Day is more important right now. According to the National Retail Federation, Americans spent over 24 billion dollars on Mother's Day, compared to only 14 billion dollars on Father's Day. Furthermore, 84 percent of people said they planned to celebrate Mother's Day, compared to 76 percent for Father's Day.

Where I worked, Mother's Day was clearly the busiest day of the year, with Thanksgiving quickly gaining a place. Every employee looks forward to this day of the year. There isn't a single moment of respite throughout the day. It's basically crazy from start to finish. Father's Day, on the other hand, occurs on a Sunday in June.

We not only devote more effort to finding the perfect gift for our mothers, but we also spend significantly more money on Mother's Day than on Father's Day.

Mother's Day spending reached an estimated $25 billion this year, according to the National Retail Federation, while Father's Day spending was "only" $16 billion.

What is the reason for this? Part of it can be attributable to the fact that Mother's Day was officially recognized considerably earlier in the United States. It was designated as a national holiday in 1914, although Father's Day was not until 1972. While the fact that Mother's Day was officially acknowledged six years before the 19th amendment was enacted is sadly ironic, it still means that the holiday had a big head start on its patriarchal counterpart.

When it comes to conventional gifts for women versus males, there is usually a price difference. For women, we tend to focus on goods like pricey jewelry, whereas for men, we revert to ties. Mother's Day, it goes to reason, is more historically marketable than Father's Day. After all, actual free will does not exist, and we are all constantly marketed to. The intentions of all holidays are skewed by capitalism.

I've had a kidney stone previously, and the pain is said to be equivalent to childbirth. I did, however, pass a little calcified mass. My mother had already passed me. To be honest, I'm not sure how birth mothers don't constantly remind their children of this truth. I wouldn't put up with any of my nonsense if I had given birth to myself.

One of the ways heteronormative standards influence views is through this. Not everyone who has given birth is a mother, and not everyone who has given birth is a mother. This distinction is critical because the miracle of life defines only some motherly relationships, not all.

Even so, whenever I consider what my mother had to go through to bring me into the world, I feel a sense of grateful guilt. I have a very large head. In terms of biology, who is my biological father? He donates his sperm. Sorry once more, dad.

If this sounds like a veiled criticism of my father, believe me when I say it isn't. My father is a decent, hardworking man who has made numerous sacrifices to support our family, but I would never say it to him. Okay, maybe I'll make it to that location before his funeral, but who knows?

My father and I have an emotional barrier between us, which I understand are rather common. That's where the term "toxic masculinity" comes into play. I, an emotionally guarded male, have never had or will ever have an emotionally vulnerable relationship with another man. It just makes me feel uneasy. Let's not talk about our sentiments; instead, let's talk about sports, and maybe an emotion or two may surface in the context of talking about touchdown dance celebrations or whatever.

This is one of the factors that makes Father's Day seem less significant to me. I'm not sure whether my father feels anything other than hatred for his favorite teams and a fondness for Werther's originals. Getting gifts for him is not only more difficult, but it is also less expressive. Gifts are concrete expressions of a person's emotions, and yearly hats just don't cut them.

I can certainly state as a straight white male that we spoil everything. After all, we are the root of the majority of the world's issues. In our increasingly liberal culture, misogyny still exists, and we have a long way to go. There is no such thing as a white history month or a men's history month because every month is both.

Men's achievements are simply less important to commemorate because we have done so for millennia. Like a good crop dusting, this applies to Father's Day, and I'm not talking about corn. Crop dusting, for those unfamiliar, is when you fart while going past someone. After you've walked through, your poisonous vapors will drift across their senses. They'll have no idea what struck them.

What I mean is that celebrating Father's Day makes me feel a little icky. While it's wonderful to honor your father figure, does he really need another day dedicated to him? The stench of patriarchal gasses lingers throughout the day, making everything smell a little like ass.

CHAPTER SIX

THE PERFECT GIFT FOR YOUR MOTHER

Mother's Day is a lovely time to honor her accomplishments.

Mothers need to be recognized for all the sacrifices they make each and every day to ensure their families are happy and healthy, whether it's taking care of their children, keeping the house clean, or making beautiful homemade meals.

Why Make Handmade Mom Gifts?

Homemade gifts may have a negative reputation that is not always justified. Some may try to convince you that handcrafted presents are "insincere" or "cheap," but we know better. She'll enjoy it if you take the effort to discover the ideal homemade present that reflects your Mom's personality.

A handmade present is the perfect complement to a thoughtful Mother's Day message. So, when you're ready to come up with the perfect idea for a thoughtful present, start with the list below.

Individualized pillow

Pillows can be customized with sweet messages and styles. Outdoor cushions with names will provide a personal touch to your patio or front porch. These cushions will liven up any spring, summer, or fall gathering as a conversation starter and a keepsake.

Make a Silhouette Brooch Create personalized brooches.

Use silhouette shapes of her children or grandkids to display at dinner parties and community gatherings, or frame them for her to enjoy at home.

Ceramic Mugs Make Great Mother's Day Gifts

Give a gift that will be used every day: a personalized cup that Mom can fill with her favorite beverage. Select a memorable photo of the two of you and a design that complements her personality. She'll think of you and your thoughtfulness every time she drinks her iced chai latte or morning orange juice.

Customized Notepads

Take heed! Make a notebook for Mom to write cards, notes, and special messages to family and friends. She'll grin every time her pen strikes the pad because your photo is on the page. She'll never miss a crucial appointment or forget to complete a task again thanks to your personalized notepad.

Stamps and cards made by hand

With an ink pad, make a unique card or souvenir. Make use of a variety of colors, such as black, pink, or orange. Add these easy touches to your Mother's Day gift, card, or wrapping paper to show Mom how much you care.

Write Mom Heartfelt Letters

Take the time to create a card to your mother that includes memories and emotional remarks about why she is precious to you. Every word you say will be filled with love and thoughtfulness, which she will notice.

Use pressed flowers, a handwritten note, and other homemade treats like cookies or chocolates to make it more personal.

Personalized monogram

Make a family sign that may be displayed inside or out. Mom would like how this symbolizes family and the affection you share. If it's an exterior piece, make sure it's sealed properly.

Soaps with scents to help Mom unwind

 Homemade scented soaps are a great gift for every mom. Because mothers put in so much effort, they deserve to relax, unwind, and soak in the tub.

Favorite Moments Can Be Turned Into Wall Art. Make a stunning wall art piece using your favorite photographs, phrases, and sayings. This sweet, handcrafted

Mother's Day present will make her smile every time she sees your thoughtful, emotional work of art.

Scarf with Style

 Crochet a scarf to complement your mother's personal style, color preferences, and clothing. Every time she wears it to work, out with friends, or at home, she'll have you close to her heart. Combine this with a cotton tote bag that she may use to shop or run errands in. If she wants to take her scarf off, she can put it in the bag.

www.ingramcontent.com/pod-product-compliance
Lightning Source LLC
Chambersburg PA
CBHW060931130726
48001CB00006B/2518